IVAN ANTIC

THE PROCESS OF REALIZATION

A DETAILED DESCRIPTION OF THE PROCESS

OF EVERY KIND OF REALIZATION,

THE LAW OF ATTRACTION,

FROM QUANTUM FIELDS AND MIND,

TO THE MATTER

Copyright © 2017 by Ivan Antic

All rights reserved.

ISBN:1543242782
ISBN-13: 978-1543242782

TABLE OF CONTENTS

	Introduction	1
1	The nature of reality	4
	1.1 The nature of energy is movement	6
	1.2 Matter does not move, information does - everything is momentary and nothing is substantial	6
	1.3 The nature of consciousness	7
2	Materialization of consciousness through the dimensions of reality	9
3	Man is a microcosm comprised of all the dimensions of nature	11
4	All the possible realities already exist simultaneously and parallel	16
5	Man's being is multidimensional because it is a reflection of the multidimensional universe	20
6	Paradigms and convictions shape our realities	21
7	Work with thoughts	23
	7.1 Thoughts and time	26
8	Work with will and energy	29
9	Work with the imagination	32
10	Work on the physical plain	34

INTRODUCTION

Tao sages in antiquity depicted the process of man's growing to his full realization as watering raised vegetable beds. The gardener doesn't flush the water onto the beds, but merely removes all obstacles in its path, enabling the water to flow freely and provide energy for the crops to yield a rich harvest.

A similar thing happens with the life energy in your body. It knows what it is supposed to do to keep your body healthy, and it will continuously do so, unless you disrupt its natural flow.

A similar thing happens with the events in your life. The same kind of life energy and consciousness in motion takes part in what you do and what happens to you. Your being is not separated from the wholeness of nature, it is not different from the one and the same energy that makes everything possible. In the totality of nature there are no boundaries, nothing is inward or outward about it, and therefore neither is your life, nor are the events of your life, your triumphs and defeats, they cannot exist separated from this wholeness.

In nature the life energy spontaneously realizes all its potential in all of its beings. Still, a majority of people shun this natural tendency and go through life feeling alienated from nature while constantly lacking fulfillment. No single reason can be found for the man failing to fulfill his true potential to its fullest, but for one: he himself is the blocking factor and keeps turning the flow toward the wrong cause. This problem is additionally exacerbated by the fact that there is a safety in numbers, or in this case, many people with the corrupt mindset, the inferior paradigms within themselves, create a system of perpetual obstacles, where consequently the obstacles become literally objective. Entire cultures get based on repression and self-inflicted feeling of guilt that further block a man from realizing his full potential.

This human characteristic to do wrong is integral part of the divine creativity. Consciousness rests on the freedom of all the possibilities. By experiencing the wrong a man acquires awareness of what is correct, and unlike plants and animals that spontaneously and automatically realize their full potential, man has a higher, objective awareness of the entire process. Objective consciousness envelops all the contradictions, including the awareness of what is wrong, not only what is right. In such a fashion, man's consciousness rises to the divine consciousness that enables the whole nature, with all its opposites and all its possibilities.

According to some Gnostic teachings the divine consciousness that enables everything further implements its act of creation, and experiences all the potentials to the fullest, by simply picking up where it left off with the growth of consciousness through both organic and non-organic world of assorted shapes, down to the plant and animal life.

This book will be based on a postulate that enhances such objective consciousness, and on understanding the manual that keeps instructing us on how to use the very consciousness that enables everything, the consciousness which is the foundation of everything.

Namely, there are many levels of working and achieving certain goals. Hard physical labor is the lowest form. You can achieve your goals, but only within its paradigm and with the physical strength involved. Using your intellect you can greatly speed up and improve your performance, but there, too, exist limitations imposed by the paradigms with which we apply ourselves to such tasks and chosen goals. Should we opt for using the consciousness itself, the consciousness which is the basis of the existence itself, which enables the very intellect and the physical realm, we then achieve our goals most directly and most efficiently.

Firstly, we will get acquainted with the nature of the reality itself, for we can do nothing unless we have, at least, some ground level knowledge of it beforehand. Afterwards, we will get acquainted with the dimensions and the proportions of reality and the way in which they are linked to our being and our actions. Then, we will learn how to shake off misconceptions and the wrong paradigms in an attempt to adopt only the ideas that will help us remove obstacles and pave the way for our creative potential.

You are most likely familiar with many how-to-succeed-in-life tips, or the law of attraction, which are all correct, however most of them are based on using consciousness and energy as though they were common knowledge, like we are completely one with the nature of reality and the influence of thoughts on this reality in terms of implementing the law of attraction. It is due to this sad fact why many people have not been very successful in their techniques.

Here we will get acquainted with the nature of objective reality, consciousness, and thoughts using the knowledge and experience of quantum physics and the Cabal, however not their abstract theories, but just the basic, practical principles, in order to use this knowledge in a much more efficient way to succeed with the law of attraction in our everyday life. (The most powerful and well-to-do people of this world are, without exception, followers of the Cabal).

Consciousness is the foundation of all the existence. If we rely on consciousness before we rely on anything else in life, then all forms of existence, all its possibilities, and all its realizations are available to us. Nothing is possible without consciousness. If this consciousness is to be used in its most rudimentary form, then it is most potent and most effective. This consciousness that enables everything is the exact same consciousness that makes us aware of things here and now, of ourselves, and of the world around us. An additional problem is that we use it to a lesser degree following a very subjective pattern. The more we grow in our comprehension of the nature of the consciousness itself and the nature of reality itself, the more loudly our actions will speak than words.

1. THE NATURE OF REALITY

At the turn of the twentieth century quantum physics made a discovery which sums up to the fact that our material reality is, in fact, a field of pure energy. This field of pure energy was later called the quantum or the universal field. It was discovered that it exists and works as a realm where everything we see in our harsh material reality has already been manifested. Quantum field stands as the hidden or implicit order in this manifested and explicit world we live in.[1] All the imminent possibilities about to take place or shape are already there.

Accordingly, the nature of reality is always one and the same, although its appearance is dual: as manifested or hidden; hidden in its quantum field in the form of pure energy, or manifested in some harsh form, or seemingly an event. Following this pattern, nothing new exists in the universe, to our perception something that expresses itself from the already existing quantum field and appearing to us for the first time merely seems novel. Everything that is manifested has already been around in its potential form. Nothing comes about from nothingness, unless it had previously been there as an option. Everything has its cause. The origin of all causes is the universal quantum field. In ancient times, it was identified in esoteric philosophy as ether or *akasha* in Sanskrit.

Consequently, your whole being, and all your living, all of the events in your life, have already existed as possibilities in the universal quantum field. The freedom of your individual consciousness is in the fact that you activated only those options that later happened to you, the ones you actualized. Possibilities are endless, but they only get actualized when certain conditions and causes are met, because this is the true nature of the physical world. Hence, causality and the freedom of choice are not conflicted per se, they interact in harmony.

It has been proved experimentally that the subatomic world of the quantum field works regardless of time and space, everything in it is interconnected, and information gets passed from one subatomic particle to another instantaneously no matter how far apart they are. In other words, in this quantum field, in the primary field of natural reality, everything is interconnected in one inextricable unity. Nature in its basic form is one and only Unity, no divisions are possible.

In accordance with this find, it has been discovered that the nature of reality corresponds to a hologram. Thus, the theory of the holographic

---

[1] David Bohm – *Wholeness And The implicate Order* (First published 1980 by Routledge & Kegan Paul).

universe emerged. It states that everything in the cosmos is connected in such a way that one tiny part contains the image of the whole.[2]

This is important for comprehending the consciousness because it sums up one obvious fact that the consciousness is the foundation of the whole nature. Every particle and every atom communicates instantaneously with all the other particles and atoms. The whole nature is one big information system which communicates instantaneously with all its seemingly divided parts.

Our nervous system serves the function of slowing down this instantaneous communication of everyone with everything, and it acts like a filter that disables the movement of information from everything in nature to our perception, it slows down the movement of the nature below the speed of light so we can only detect the reality that exists slower than the speed of light and in linear time. The nervous system is not the mechanism that serves the purpose of creating or emitting the consciousness, but of slowing it down to a sufficient degree so we could communicate and exist in this three-dimensional physical reality, in which we live.

If it were not for this, we would be lost in the totality of nature, it would be impossible for us to exist like this. However, our nervous system does not play the role of a brake because our consciousness is far greater than our brains. If we were to use nothing but our nervous system, we would be hardened materialists, and our perception would be like that of animals. For most people this is not the case. We can use our consciousness to a far greater extent, and alter our reality, and not necessarily our own only, but that of our environment as well. Our consciousness is, in effect, the same consciousness that constitutes the quantum field. This higher capacity of our consciousness is often referred to as the divine mind, or is determined to be our connection to God, and only recently did it receive the epithet of quantum as in mind or thinking, the functioning of the quantum consciousness. It will be referred to as only "consciousness", or the "consciousness of our soul" here, and it will be understood that our soul is an individual expression of the divine consciousness that enables everything, that enables the existence itself.

---

[2] On the universal field in modern physics see Lynne McTaggart: *The Field: The Quest for the Secret Force of the Universe* (2003). On the holographic paradigm see Michael Talbot: *The Holographic Universe*, 1991. On understanding and connecting the consciousness of the quantum field with the holographic universe see Gregg Braden: *The Divine Matrix: Bridging Time, Space, Miracles, and Belief*, 2006.

1.1 The nature of energy is movement

If the basis of everything is energy, what is that energy, then? The word is derived from Greek where it stands for "being in motion". In other words, it is vibration. Vibration is based on electromagnetic polarization. Polarization is the starting point for everything, it instigates the movement of everything. The movement is energy. That is why the energy is always emitted through some motion or movement.

The energy is vibration, and the most fundamental vibration of nature is the one of the quantum field. It is comprised of vibration alone. For this reason, it is said that this is the field of pure energy. These vibrations are also called the quantum fluctuation.

Starting from the initial subtle differences in vibrations, that is the quantum fluctuation, in accordance with the model of fractal geometry, gradually bigger and more complex differences in the energy of vibrations are constructed, or assorted vibration energetic structures and creations are made. This further results in the creation of even more complex forms that manifest themselves as particles, or the clusters of particles and as atoms, that get attracted to or repelled by other objects, which correlates with the nature of their vibrations, thus creating even bigger shapes such as molecules, and the final outcome should be something we can see as a physical form, a living being, or some event.

This is how all things and manifestations are brought about, from the finest vibrations of energy down to the harsh physical world we are able to detect with our senses. The foundation of everything is energy. All the differences we are able to perceive here, for instance between metal and plastic, are essentially just the differences in vibrations on a subatomic level, particles that constitute metal vibrate in one way, whereas with plastic they vibrate in a different way. That is all. There are no differences in matter, since nothing is material to begin with, everything is energy that keeps vibrating in one way or another.

1.2 Matter does not move, information does - Everything is momentary and nothing is substantial

If the essence of energy is movement, what is that which actually moves? Only information. Wave is synchronized oscillating which, in turn, induces yet another instance of oscillation. Matter does not get transferred though the wave, meaning a particle through space, only information does, which will correspondingly induce some different information as a result. All rough shapes are formed on the basis of subtle information. Like a wave on the ocean. It is not one and the same wave we see traveling on the surface of the ocean, but the water goes up and down in such a synchronized way that it appears to be nothing but that one wave. Similarly, nothing is substantial, matter that moves through time and space simply does not exist. All such forms are merely a momentary state of certain vibrations. Everything exists following this principle of momentariness.

1.3 The nature of consciousness

Any shape of some momentary energy vibration represents information at the same time. All the movement of information in nature is simultaneous with the movement of energy. Information modulates and directs the forming and the impact of energy. Energy has no way of knowing what to do with itself without the presence of information which directs it and gives it shape, it is information that is embedded in the very form and movement. There is no difference between the shape and the information. The essence of all information is in the awareness of the meaning of all the information, in making sense of action. There is no information without the awareness that comprehends it, for which it is aimed. This means that consciousness is the foundation of everything, it is the foundation of energy vibrations, as well as the foundation of information that modulates the impact of energy. Indeed, if consciousness were not the foundation of informational movement of energy, neither life nor the cosmos would exist, only chaos would be possible. Consciousness gives meaning to everything that exists.

In the natural order of reality consciousness comes first, then energy, then all the forms energy creates. Consciousness is the foundation of all the biological and chemical processes, and the physical reality itself. Nothing exists outside consciousness. Neither our being, nor the events that constitute our destiny.

Every shape in nature exists only thanks to the conscious intention to be there. The Earth you stand on, your body, every shape in nature, anything you see around yourself, it all exists owing to the conscious intention to exist in such a shape. Mercedes car G class has come into existence because somebody applied their will consciously to manufacture it, and, in the same way, every flower exists thanks to the conscious intention.

This consciousness that enables everything has been established long ago to be the divine consciousness, and has been identified with the idea of God. However, the original idea has been dispersed into various religious forms where some abstract metaphors have been given more significance than the meaning they are supposed to convey.

The true meaning of God mind remained clear only to individual dedicators and secret societies, it was turned into esoteric knowledge. Here we shall get acquainted with it through the teaching of Cabal and the process of materialization of consciousness into the rough physical shape.

For now, let us keep this important fact in mind: this divine consciousness that enables everything, and which is the essence of the quantum field and all the energy, to which all the meaning of all the information that direct the life energy is meant for, is the very consciousness which enables us to become aware of who and what we are here and now, and to have the full awareness of all our thoughts and deeds. It is also our consciousness. We only use it to a lesser degree. We may increase the power of applying our consciousness onto our life in one way only: by understanding how consciousness works, by understanding all the dimensions it affects us through, and by taking responsibility for the energy we consciously spend, in order for us to do what we do.

Before we go any further we must understand how this limited consciousness we are able to perform with here came into being. The divine consciousness emanates all its possibilities in the form of individual shaping. Using this principle it was able to express itself individually through the monads of consciousness known to us here as the souls. Our soul is, basically, one individual monad or a fragment of the divine consciousness. In the process of emanating further it splits, diversifies and contracts itself into what we are familiar with here as our "higher mind" or "higher I". Finally, this divine consciousness using our souls shapes our physical body and acts within it as a physical mind or ego. It is the type of consciousness we have in this world here and now. It is a tiny reflection of the consciousness in nature. It is connected by means of our higher mind with the consciousness of the soul, and the divine consciousness. One and the same consciousness keeps interacting within itself, there is not a multitude of consciousnesses, one should simply be made aware of how it branches out and splits itself into a variety of shapes.

2. MATERIALIZATION OF CONSCIOUSNESS THROUGH THE DIMENSIONS OF REALITY

In all esoteric traditions the nature of reality gets described using these elements - earth, water, fire, air.

These elements symbolically represent the dimensions of reality. Cabala possesses the most detailed description where these elements are depicted in the teaching of *tetragrammaton*. *Tetragrammaton* is a four letter word JHVH made up of the Hebrew letters Yod, He, Vau, He.

Jehovah, "the god's name", was derived from it to serve its purpose with illiterate folk who were not aware of the esoteric truth that this formula, JHVH, represents the four-pole principle of the universal creation of the world through the four elements: earth, water, fire and air. At the same time, it represents all the dimensions of creation, the four dimensions of reality by means of which everything in nature gets manifested and materialized, starting from information down to the rough material form.

In religious stories we are being told that God made man in his image, which means that man is actually a microcosm, that in a man's being there are all the big cosmic laws and principles condensed; man is the cosmos in miniature. It actually points to the holographic model of existence of all the life in universe, where every tiny fragment contains the pattern of the wholeness, since nothing is detached in nature.

Above these four elements or principles there is an additional one which is called ether, in the East it is called *akasha*, which means space. Ether enables all other elements, the same way space enables everything into existence. Space is the primary condition for the existence of everything else. Therefore, this primary condition has been accurately called *akasha* or space. Hence, we have the following order in the dimensions of reality:

Ether
Air
Fire
Water
Earth

Air, fire, water, and earth symbolically represent the universal principles of the process of emanation of everything. Ether or *akasha* is the immaterial and irreducible principle of the extensibility of their emanation. Likewise, ether corresponds to the quantum field in physics.

Different dimensions of consciousness in a man's being can be divided according to the elements in the following way.

The pure presence of the consciousness and alertness belong to the element of ether (*akasha*).

The element of air marks one's inspiration and ideas, awareness that is formed and that keeps forming ideas, thoughts, and mental patterns.

The element of fire is an area of mental activity, exchange of ideas, preparation and assertion of energy for their realization, expressing one's will in accordance with one's mind set.

Water symbolizes the area where from a multitude of possibilities one specific idea is chosen and with the emotional empathizing it is maintained in one constant, concrete, and visible form for focusing the energy, which, eventually, gets realized on the area of earth as the physical experience.

Take, for example, car manufacturing. In the element of air it is present only as a sheer idea of more effective travel; on the level of fire all of the possible models of transport vehicles and vessels ever made are imminent; on the water plain one specific model has been selected and mapped out, and with the genuine and persistent vesting of energy on those higher plains by adding human labor it gets turned into reality on the earth plain. Everything that happens in the physical world follows this footpath, getting to know it better increases one's potential for creativity. Everything we concoct in the world of ideas and imagination (air and fire) and form strong emotional ties with on astral (water) is materialized here on earth.

It is important to perceive that ether, which corresponds to the quantum field, is the foundation of everything, and it goes beyond it, much like the space that enables everything. In our being, the microcosm, that is at the same time our essential consciousness we are present in all the dimensions with, owing to which we can be aware of all the dimensions and of this entire process of materialization. If consciousness were not above it all, we would not be able to become aware of this.

Other authors have explained, in great detail, the significance of thoughts, strong desire and vivid imagination in the law of attraction. Only with the deeper understanding of the dimensions of reality and the principle of *tetragrammaton* can you begin to realize why it is so important, what the meaning and the wider context of the impact of thoughts, desire and imagination in the process of materialization of every idea is.

3. MAN IS A MICROCOSM COMPRISED OF ALL THE DIMENSIONS OF NATURE

We, human beings, were made "in God's image", that is as microcosm by being made up of all the dimensions of nature: from ether or the pure consciousness of the self; from the element of air or the mental body and thoughts; from the element of fire which gives us intention and strong will power; from the element of water which gives us emotions and imagination; and from the element of earth or the physical body.

For this reason we can exist on earth, to feel (water), to have our own will (fire), and to think (air). The dimensions of the whole nature that are focused in our being enable this for us.

The pure consciousness of the self is from *akasha* or ether or the universal quantum field, which with the progressive compounding of the possibilities of the consciousness of the self, through mind or the mental body, the body of will and the emotional body, has shaped the physical body we possess. This is how we have the physical body, the feelings, the will and mind. This is the way in which we have come to forget the consciousness of our soul.

Man's being is the tetragrammaton.
Universe creates and becomes aware of itself in all its dimensions through the man's being.

All other beings exist in a limited way, they don't have all the dimensions in them, they are restricted to one dimension alone, and to a certain manner of perception.

On the level of the element of air there are all the potential possibilities of existence, which are timelessly compressed in ether or the quantum field, they are expressed as pure ideas, possibilities, they are expressed in us in the form of thoughts, as well. All objects exist there in the form of ideas.

In the element of fire ideas are formed into energy, they are recognized as energy; it is expressed in us as an intention or will to realize some idea, so that it does not remain purely abstract; all the objects in the element of fire already exist in the form of pure energy, intention, or the will to realize a certain idea.

In the element of water an idea united with the will and intention starts to take shape in the world of imagination, on astral, which is associated with our emotional body. All objects exist there in astral form, where we can visualize them with the tiniest of detail.

When all these previous elements are added together, an object which previously existed as an idea, energy and astral form, materializes on the element of earth as a concrete physical object, a thing or an event. Only then can we take it in our hands and touch it. Like our smartphone, for instance.

All these elements exist and have a combined impact on us. Once we are aware of this, when we see a certain object, we also automatically get the idea and thought which identifies it, when we took it in our hands for the first time we thought: this is my smartphone. We don't repeat that later, but we take it for granted. This is what we do each and every time we see an object for the first time, we identify it with our thoughts, we design it, we name it.

It already exists in the world of ideas as well as on the physical plain. It is one and the same object, but only because the nature of reality exists in multiple dimensions does it split and emit itself through those dimensions. In the element of air smartphone is in our minds in the form of thought, whilst we are holding it as a physical object in our hands. That is an identical phenomenon which only the differences in dimensions split into an outer object and an inner thought. It is a thought in us, and externally it is a physical object.

For one simple fact that the thought in us is as real as the external objects. Only different dimensions split them and make them appear different.

In order to realize our ideas we should just become aware and harmonize all the processes they go through from the origin in thoughts to materialization.

Since man is a *tetragrammaton*, because all the dimensions are compressed in him, only in a man all the consciousness which unites this entire process of creation and materialization can take place. At the same time, for the same reason, only a man can experience the illusion that those processes are detached.

Our capacity for attracting and realizing things lies in this process of performing things from the idea to the material realization of that idea.

Every idea can be realized and materialized (in the element of earth) only if we put all four principles together and put them to practice following the obvious steps, sticking to the idea persistently and treating it like a goal (air), passionately pursuing it (fire), seeing it as already finalized in our mind's eye (water).

Performing in the element of earth represents all the physical labor it takes to accept the realization of an idea we had previously created in the higher dimensions. The designed will undoubtedly reach us provided we showed dedication on higher plain, but the physical part of the job can only be done by us if we are to receive it when it comes.

One should act on every plain in accordance with the characteristics of that specific plain, likewise, on the physical plain we must be tuned with the corresponding vibration of the physical plain, and that is the physical labor. The desired object will not fly to us by way of telekinesis as in a fairy-tale. We will need to clear the field and open the roads up, and maybe even organize practical means of physical transportation.

If we imagine one thing in our mind's eye and invest our energy in something else, interference is inevitable, we will not be able to realize anything on the physical plain. Consistency has always been the rudimentary cause of any form of realization. However, consistency must function on all four levels of realization. Consistency on one level alone is not sufficient, such as in thoughts or wishes, if our vision remains unclear, and there is not the amount of labor to follow. Mere understanding or the awareness of the entire process can bring the four elements together focused towards one universal goal. Consequently, the awareness of the functioning of this entire process is crucial when applying the law of attraction.

When we are aware of this whole process we can make any idea come true. Anyone who has practically applied an idea has done so in the way described here, by utter consistency on all four levels of realization. Anyone who has failed to realize his ideas has, evidently, sabotaged this process on one of the levels, by not succeeding in harmonizing and interconnecting it on all the levels; he, mistakenly led himself to believe they can be realized in different way, and not in the way described here. Most definitely, he has falsely remained under the illusion that other people are to blame, or, perhaps, some alien set of circumstances or weird forces.

Outside forces do exist and can be very powerful, but man is a *tetragrammaton*, a microcosm, and all the principles of creation are within him. All that is required is the consciousness which will actualize all the processes through him.

As a matter of fact, for any kind of realization only one quality is needed - the right awareness - the awareness of the entire process on all four levels, the awareness that interconnects all the levels. The moment we consciously interconnect all four elements of the process of realization, and remain equally consistent on each one, that moment our thought comes true.

That is our innate ability which we constantly use, it always happens, nothing happens otherwise. Our thoughts create our life. Look at the world around you. What do you see? Apart from the nature itself, everything you see has been man-made, all the buildings and technology, following the trail of this principle of creation starting from the ideas and ending in its realization.

It most commonly happens unconsciously, hence the negative result. Everything materializes this way, by means of these four principles, and that as a consequence has that all the bad things happened following the same principles. Our propensity for investing sincere energy and fervor into our negative thoughts is far greater than investing in our top projects. As an outcome bad things happen to us sooner rather than later. This constitutes one of the many laws of nature: creation requires more energy than destruction.

It is far easier to break a smartphone than to make it. The point is that one needs to encapsulate all four processes described here for the creation to take place, and for the destruction it takes only one broken link connecting one of the levels. Likewise, we are not alone, there is a collective impact, the presence of other people who also leave their mark unconsciously, with adverse outcome, therefore, over a period of time various material and social environment get created that objectively hinder our growth, and our good living.

All it takes is for us to grasp our intentions and mental patterns on the most refined level, in its original condition, all our convictions, and our paradigms with which we access reality, for it is those that shape our physical reality. Our original idea will shape the remainder on the lower levels, our will and imagination as well as our physical reality.

For this obvious reason we ought not complain about our inferior accomplishments and the given physical reality, but should rather divert our attention to the primary impulse which set everything in motion. It is relatively pointless to try to upgrade our emotions, imagination, or our expression of will and energy; a wiser option would be to retrace our footprints back to the beginning of the initial impulse, from the awareness of the mental mindset that instigates all the processes, and make a conscious effort to harmonize ourselves with it. One should always start from the beginning, from the very source, and preferably avoid dealing with consequences and symptoms.

On the highest level of creation, in God's consciousness, there was quite an outstanding paradigm and the intention to manifest all the possibilities. Naturally, the purity of ideas got dispersed on the declining path to the lower levels and got pretty distorted by the time it reached man.

Divine consciousness modified the entire cosmos and all the existence through its individual monads or souls. In their memories prior to birth,[3]

---

[3] Michael Newton: *Journey of Souls, Case Studies of Life Between Lives*, 1994.

in the hypnotic regression, we receive information that our souls created all forms of life, plant and animal species, before they got incarnated in this body.

At that point they were rehearsing creativity. They had the assistance of the divine consciousness which enables everything, for they, too, have their origin in the divine consciousness. Additionally, from the hypnotic regression we receive reports of our soul being the chief designer of the current life and body we live in. It is only a fragment of the truth.

Actually, we, as souls, participated in the creation of the universe itself, the Earth, the nature, and all of our body's environment and set of circumstances. It makes no sense to believe that we created this body, and not all the living conditions for it, especially being aware of the fact, that it resides in the holographic universe where absolutely nothing is separated from the wholeness of the nature.

The earth we walk on, the water we drink, the air we breathe, all of these things we have created by ourselves for ourselves – naturally not with this little lost ego of ours we are now, identified with the body, but as souls, as the structural parts of the divine consciousness that enables everything.

When you come to understand this seriously, the law of attraction will be much clearer and easier.

4. ALL THE POSSIBLE REALITIES ALREADY EXIST SIMULTANEOUSLY AND PARALLEL

The described process of creation of everything from an idea to the material reality happens momentarily, rather than during a course of time. Only observed from the point of human experience it appears to stretch over a period of time. In the real world a thought of an object and the object itself are one and the same thing, it simply happens that the nature of reality which consists of the four familiar principles (or dimensions) keeps them apart. This is why we have the existence which consists of the information about the objects and the objects themselves. If it were not so, there would be no objective world, everything would be one diffuse unity. A man's experience splits it and it is the only thing that can creatively put them back together again.

We have already stated that the quantum field is a place where the entire existence is joint in one timeless unity, in which everything that has been or will be manifested already exists, so basically there is nothing new that could take place. We have said, accordingly, that this unity exists based on the principle of the holograph, where every tiny detail contains the principle of the wholeness.

Now we must introduce yet another great principle so as to be able to comprehend how all of this can function. It is the principle of *parallel realities*. Since the foundation of nature is one timeless unity, it is evident that whatever comes out of this unity cannot be a myriad of separate objects existing in time. In other words, God does not waste time on linear creation. He creates everything he can create and has already created, but not all of it belongs to one reality exclusively. All potential realities coexist in parallel.

Those are not some illusive other dimensions that quantum physicists confuse you with. Parallel dimensions are simply the ones that constitute our life experience.

For example, you grew up in a dysfunctional family, with divorced parents, which greatly affected you. You had psychological problems and difficulty in adjusting to your environment, community and the challenges in life.

That is one reality.

Afterwards, you used your intelligence and learnt a thing or two about psychology, you were able to see that your situation wasn't unique, that it had its cause, so you decided to do something useful with your life, after all. You improved your attitude, upgraded your school report, and made a conscious choice to go on to a higher education in order to give yourself a better start in life. You paved the way for making something of yourself, to lead a successful life, much better than that of your parents.

That is the choice of a different reality.

However, you still haven't completely left the first reality behind. You are forced to revisit it. You should know that realities interchange frequently, and they affect one another in numerous ways. You still live in your old neighborhood with the problematic kids, some of them are maybe even your relatives, who are fixed to the first reality, and who define your first reality.

The people you live with and who constitute your first reality are still around and may affect or hinder the manifestation of your second reality, and its realization. The more you persist in your new reality, and that is the reality of an up and coming individual, the more the persons from your former reality will begin to fade, and disappear from your life eventually.

You may see them again, but they will not have the same hold over you they previously had, back in the day when you shared the identical reality with them. Mental and emotional independence from the specific influences is the feature of disassociating from reality which generates the influence. It is often necessary to distance ourselves from the individuals who belong to the former reality we wish to abandon, because their interference may be too strong. However, the strength of our character is best reflected in the fact that we change despite the temptations of the environment.

If we were to flee constantly from all the obstructions, we would not get far in our growth. Understanding the alternate realities may be of most help to us in resisting the temptations of the environment. The strengthening of our mental and emotional independence is exactly the way in which we can change our realities. This independence cannot be strengthened by running away from a certain reality, because by running we acknowledge its power over us, we can only transform it by understanding it through experience. Understanding has always been the only way of surpassing all the limitations.

The way in which all the potential possibilities for shaping any object exist in the quantum field, the same way ***all the potential life realities already exist*** in a timeless manner as sheer possibilities. It is up to our awareness which of the realities we get to choose and how we organize the transition between them.

When we apply the law of attraction we do not create a new reality but consciously select the already existing alternative reality, and

following the principle of tetragrammaton we realize it, i.e. actualize it.

Firstly, we form an idea of it, then invest all our energy into its realization, we visualize a specific desired outcome and the desired reality as though they were here, until, at one point, they, finally, become our physical reality.

We do not create a different reality - it already exists, everything has been created and is there in the parallel reality - we only select it and cross over to it. We merely actualize it with our awareness, we transfer it from the potential or implicit state into actualized or the explicit state.

The tiny changes and transitions from one reality to another happen all the time. To some limited extent they happen to us, too, on occasion of changing the state of our consciousness, or in the change of our mood. We don't detect them as modifications of one reality in correlation with another, most commonly, those alterations are so slight that we maintain the continuity of one reality albeit with minor oscillations.

It can be argued that there are multiple I's in us, and that every single one represents one reality. However, sometimes strong blow hits us, and it changes our personality permanently. Likewise, negative change can also occur, and they modify our I's into fragmenting so that one I has no knowledge of the other ones. It happens thanks to the fact that our reality is multidimensional and all the realities act together simultaneously and as parallel options. Such nature of reality sometimes overpowers our consciousness and maintains the continuity of one reality.

The crucial bit in this whole matter is that there exists a consciousness that surpasses and brings together all the realities, in the form of space that supports the existence of everything. This consciousness is our essential consciousness, the consciousness of our soul. It is above all the realities and all the change. The very fact that we can testify of all the realities and their change here proves that we possess the awareness which goes beyond any reality. Only if we are above something can we be objectively aware of it. The essence of consciousness is in its power to rise above everything.

Consciousness is the core of the total existence and it is always available. It can be so only because the existence is momentary and unsubstantial and owing to the fact that it resides in the parallel realities. If consciousness had to travel through time and space it would require an enormous amount of energy and time, therefore, no momentary conscious communication would be a possibility in the entire existence. However, it exists, and it has been proved beyond doubt.

Our primary goal is to ascertain our true consciousness, and to implement it in our daily performance, in the surpassing of any reality, in order to surpass consciousness which it is identified with, and conditioned by a specific reality. Only with this type of freedom and objective consciousness can we begin to change our realities.

The only way for some reality to perpetuate is for the consciousness to be identified with it. Once we discover that we are the primary consciousness, we will cease to be the slaves of any given reality.

Let us bring to mind one simple fact that consciousness is the essence of the entire existence, and that absolutely nothing can exist without it. All it takes for us to create our realities is to accept the natural facts of life. Why is it so hard?

5. MAN'S BEING IS MULTIDIMENSIONAL BECAUSE IT IS A REFLECTION OF THE MULTIDIMENSIONAL UNIVERSE

It is hard to accept all the facts of nature because we neither use all our potential, nor all our energy in all the dimensions of our existence.

Namely, it is imperative to stress that parallel realities are not merely modifications of our life style or the current mood, something we end up utilizing or not. *Parallel realities exist concretely, as distinct universes.* However, we cannot switch from one reality to another at will while we are still in this body and mind. We do not possess enough energy or presence of consciousness to be able to affect that. (There are spiritual practices that enable such achievement, but they are not the subject here.)

Transition between the parallel universes would hardly be practical for the kind of life as we know it. If such transition would be made easy, there would be total chaos. Consciousness would not have its continuity in our body. Actually, this complete transition from one reality to another naturally happens to us in the experience known to us as death and new birth. But the heart of the matter is, man should go through it with full awareness and willfully carry out here and now what spontaneously occurs, what reality indeed is.

Our mood swings, the shifting of our I's, various states of awareness and the modifications of reality we live in, are very vague and distant reflections of the multitude of parallel universes.

Knowing the fact that parallel universes are in existence we are able to rationalize our parallel thoughts, feelings, and the opportunity of change between them.

Universe is a holograph, everything reflects itself in everything.

We ourselves are multidimensional beings because we are reflections of the multidimensional universe.

Our ability to change our thoughts and use them to create different ideas and preconceptions which will take shape in a certain life situation, is just a distant reflection of the reality of the multidimensional universe where all the possibilities coexist parallel.

In this body we have sufficient energy and awareness only to be able to deal with our thoughts, with our feelings and will, as well as the body, and in such a microcosm of our life we modify situations and events with all the given limitations of time and space.

Let's see how we can apply this in practice.

6. PARADIGMS AND CONVICTIONS SHAPE OUR REALITIES

If in the foundation of existence lies complete oneness, where can we place the law of attraction, and what can we attract if we already exist in the holographic universe, if we are a microcosm ourselves?

If our goal is to attract something we want and avoid something we do not want, we are merely removing the wrong paradigms with which we have restricted ourselves in an unfavorable way. Like the gardener who waters his vegetable beds. In that aspiration we do not even deal with the outside world, we just change ourselves and raise awareness of the process.

Being under the illusion that we are changing some external situation we actually change ourselves, we perfect ourselves in this whole process. What we want to attract, some promise of a better life, already exists as a parallel reality, there is no need to drag it and create as something new in the outside world, we should just get rid of the current reality we have imprisoned ourselves in with our thoughts, concepts and convictions.

The way in which consciousness creates a certain reality, and gives it strength to survive, is to be identified with its patterns. This identification happens within us in the form of convictions, the rudimentary ones, that are deeper than the everyday reality of the mind we use, the convictions that spring up only in an event of the altered state of mind. Actually, if the consciousness did not possess this power of identification, the existence would disperse into a diffuse and shapeless oneness, the world as we know it would not exist. Therefore, it is not a negative concept, nothing could be further from the truth, we should just understand the wider context and the meaning of it all.

Our very birth in this world is a paradigm of ours, our conviction and the pattern of our soul's consciousness, which we took on before being born. Everything we have gone through in life are mind patterns, and those of the consciousness, spiked with various paradigms, not just in us, but in others, too. We are not alone in this world, there is a collective impact and the principle of vagueness. It is necessary for the game to be real, as opposed to mere acting out.

According to the *tetragrammaton* the process of any realization starts from the finer to the coarser, from the element of air or the world of ideas, down to the earth and material realization. The world of ideas is the source of our life reality. In order to change the reality of our life we must start from this finest level, from the very source. It is impossible to change reality from a lower level, with the old pattern still in charge.

The origin of thought is the closest to the origin of everything, to the quantum field itself, to *akasha* or ether, where in all the potential possibilities are contained and wherefrom all the energy for existence comes. This is why mental patterns have the biggest propensity for creation, all the other realizations on all the other lower plains are directly linked to them. In order to gain this perfectly accurate and objective insight into the process of every creation, and in order to get all the energy for any creation, we always have to rely on the origin of all the processes, the origin of thoughts, of the very mind itself. This origin we experience as the pure consciousness of the self, as awareness of the pure existence, and as bliss. A circle has only one dot for its center, all the other dots deviate from the ideal center. If we know that our being and our life is a circle, all other dots except for our center tend to oscillate and change position. Only the center is fixed and independent of any change, only the central point is equally distant from any other point, from our existence, and that is why it is always readily available.

This center is actually the holographic model of the entire circle. If our consciousness is on the verge of the circle of our existence, facing outward, it then moves in identification with all the constant changes of the state, as in turning of a wheel, sometimes on top, and sometimes on the bottom, sometimes exalted and sometimes humiliated, successful or unsuccessful. Only when it is fixed at the center of the entire existence, only then is it immobile, and always readily available, only from that point can an objective insight into everything that is be possible.

To free ourselves from the old paradigms and convictions means to put ourselves in the center of our being, the existence itself, and from there we automatically get the right insight into the reality and every realization possible. Only from the focal center are we able to get the correct insight, it manifests automatically on that spot because our center is equally distant from every other point of existence, which, according to the holographic model, means that it contains within itself every other point in the possibility of existence. From any other peripheral point our insight is conditioned and incomplete, depending on the data we currently possess and which are always limited, and depending on our accumulated knowledge. Our center already contains all the knowledge because it contains the entire circle of knowledge.

When we truly understand that everything rests on the paradigms and convictions, from the original mind pattern, then this very understanding will help us to liberate ourselves from every misconception, from every wrong paradigm. There is no other way of changing the paradigms and convictions than comprehending their true nature.

7. WORK WITH THOUGHTS

Thoughts in our given order belong to the element of air. The element of air is right beneath ether. Since ether corresponds to the universal quantum field it consists of all the hidden potentials for existence, all the dimensions, and all the realities. This means that thoughts are the information field which is the closest, in all aspects, to the quantum field of all the potential possibilities. To sum up, it is as thoughts emanate from the quantum field, the ether.

What is actually going on there?

What do thoughts do?

Quite simply, when one frequency is shaped from the universal quantum field (and they get shaped constantly in a multitude of ways, there is nothing else they do) it becomes information. It becomes an idea or a thought.

An idea becomes an idea when it is recognized as such in its content and sense with the full awareness, and then its essence is revealed as energy first, that becomes will, i.e. the element of fire. This way thoughts become intentions for further shaping and action. In order to become concrete they must descend to a more consistent form, to some image that reflects a design or an idea. When information or thought joins forces with energy we, then, get feelings.

The element of water, which represents the astral world or the world of imagination, is the world where our dreams take place. It is the world we go to when we are experiencing astral projection, but it is also the world which, for the first time, gives a visible shape to our thoughts, an image that may materialize on the physical plain, in the element of earth, in our physical reality as our physical reality.

Therefore, this entire process starts from the very vibrations of the quantum field (ether), from the energy that becomes information, which consciously recognizes itself as energy and becomes idea or thought (air). United with energy, i.e. recognized as energy, thought becomes will or intention (fire). When information joins with energy it becomes intention. And, we know that energy is filled with feelings. It can morph into this only if it takes on some shape or content (water) colored with the deepest feelings.

Accordingly, the thoughts are the most original information with which the movement of energy of the quantum field is manifested in shaping our physical reality. We select one physical reality with our thoughts that will later be realized. Everything is already there in the universal quantum field of all the potential possibilities. Man's mind is nothing but a trigger that activates a specific reality.

This is the reason why thoughts have the biggest creative power. They are the starting point of everything.

Still, this would be the description of an ideal state. The problem is that our thoughts are not always conscious and pure, we do not understand their nature and that is why they are mixed with the astral content of our subconsciousness (water) and the basic will or intent (fire), that supersedes our alert mind, which we only use when we function in reality in the physical body (earth). It is all very mixed up and this confusion constitutes our everyday life. Thoughts affect the body, the body affects the thoughts, will affects the thoughts and the body, the thoughts affect the will, where as feelings and emotions interconnect all of that into a psychotic reality of modern living.

Spontaneous, or more briefly, unconscious interference of all of these influences and levels is the key reason for our not being the masters of our thoughts, our will and energy, our feelings, or for that matter our entire being. Since we are not the masters of our being, we are neither the masters of our life or the environment. That is because our being and our environment are one and the same in this holographic universe.

The first step towards their awakening is their distinction, comprehension of all the levels and the dimensions where all the information of the universal quantum field is manifested, through all four elements. In other words, in the wholeness of our being.

Therefore, working with thoughts can be reduced to comprehending what they are. They are ideas and contents, the very thing that points in the direction of meaning. Thus, working with thoughts boils down to comprehension, making sense of the thoughts themselves and where they originate from.

Understanding thoughts is possible only by understanding the consciousness that is aware of them, by enhancing our self-conscious. The more we are aware of ourselves, the more we can be objectively aware of our own thoughts. Our self-consciousness is always more extensive than all the contents of all the thoughts. It is essential for understanding the thoughts and reaching the self-consciousness in which the thoughts themselves are objects just like everything else is in nature, the most refined objects at that; thoughts are the activity of nature on its finest, informative level.

Thoughts are nature in the form of information. Everything we see externally as the manifested form of nature is at the same time information in our mind, a thought. We are the *tetragrammaton*, we with our multidimensional being enable the shape and content, the activity and the meaning, the inner and the outer to connect in us. This merging is possible only because we split them at the same time.

By means of thoughts nature identifies and constitutes itself. Not a single thought is ours. We are just a convenient place where thought information of the existence itself compresses, intersects, and reaches the point of self-awareness. We are the consciousness that witnesses our thoughts, that understands their meaning, and because of that we may change and direct their meaning and realization.

We can be objectively aware of thoughts only because our consciousness enables the existence of the quantum field from which all the information i.e. thought vibrations emanate. This field is identified as ether, and in the eastern esoteric tradition it is also known as *akasha*. This word also means space.

Space enables any form of existence, from the finest to the coarsest. In the same fashion, consciousness can be aware of absolutely everything, from the finest to the coarsest. Therefore, the original consciousness is compatible with the space that enables everything else. This space, ether, this *akasha*, this quantum field of all potential possibilities is not some abstract microcosm – it is this space we live in here and now, the cosmic space we share with the whole planet Earth. This entire space has contracted itself in our human being so that through the process of *tetragrammaton*, all the existing dimensions can emanate themselves in all their possibilities and come to the full awareness of themselves.

Yet another aspect of thoughts should be known: they are identical with the way in which the entire existence communicates. The entire existence is woven into one giant information field, everything communicates with everything momentarily. It has been discovered that our genes communicate among themselves momentarily, independently of time and space, using the same linguistic rules our everyday language and speech are based on. It is logical that our language is based on the communication principles of the entire nature.

That explains how and why our thoughts, mental patterns, prayers, curses, and our very words function. We can heal with words and thoughts, we can change the functioning of our body with them, because our thoughts and words communicate directly with our genes, which use the same linguistic rules. We can have an impact and change our environment. This proves that mind patterns are not innocuous at all. They are the most powerful thing in the physical universe. Thoughts are the most refined modification of the quantum energy in this emergent cosmos, the type of energy that enables the cosmos itself. They are the starting point of everything. ("In the beginning was the Word", John 1.1)

When we learn to apply this consciously and creatively, we have learnt the art of creating phenomena.

To simplify the act of working with thoughts: it can be reduced to introducing awareness into the way we think and the things we imagine. It will, eventually, determine everything else in our life.

Hence, let's start doing it consciously. This brings forth a new culture to our thinking. Just because thoughts shift momentarily we are tricked into thinking that this will have no real consequences for us. Thoughts are of little importance only if they remain in their element, the air, as sheer ideas, if they never manage to connect to all the other elements, will, imagination and physical deeds.

The freedom of the momentariness of thoughts makes it possible to design anything and everything from all the aspects and options, however the essence of the wholeness of the existence is momentary, oscillatory action and therefore, our thoughts are on the same wavelength with the essence of existence. This brings us to the obvious notion that we must be responsible for our thoughts. Acquiring responsibility in this area is the essence of working with thoughts.

All the unfavorable conditions in our life were designed in the same manner with our thoughts, albeit subconsciously. All favorable conditions in our life we design consciously. Awareness is the only difference between the good and the evil in human existence.

Our work with thoughts in the implementation of the law of attraction lies in the fact that we must carefully design the best option of reality we wish to create. It will be in the present time as though it were already here. We should disconnect from our environment and our activities on a daily basis as often as possible, and create a mental image in our mind's eye repeatedly for at least a few minutes. We shall see in the following chapters that this should be accompanied by emotions and imagination.

7.1 Thoughts and time

There is yet another important detail we must reconsider carefully about thoughts: time. In the quantum field there is no time because in it everything already is, and nothing should become. When a vibration is generated from it, a thought, it must exist separately, because it is unique. This way it renders the illusion of linear time, as long as we think that for us there is something before (the origin of this thought), and something after. For every conscious subject something is within reach and something is very far away. This is the nature of the three-dimensional world we live in. But at the base of everything, everything already is, nothing becomes new, which means there is no time. This means that fundamental reality that makes everything possible is timelessly here and now, that there is no past and no future.

This leads us to the elementary rule of the law of attraction: in order to act from the level of true reality which enables everything, when we create a certain reality in our thoughts, we must create it independently of time and space, which means it should never be done in (the undesired) past or (the desired) future, but always in the present, as though it had already manifested itself as the reality for us.

It practically means that when we mentally define a desired reality, in the shortest and clearest way, as a formula, it must be expressed in the present tense, as the description of the present reality – although the old reality still lives on. This is the essence of our work: to supersede, albeit briefly, the current reality, and to create the desired state in thoughts as though it were actually here.

We don't create a new reality, we just swap it for a different one. A real problem may arise as to how to cross over from one reality onto a different one. For as long as we have the grip over one we cannot enter another. The subtlest way of sticking to one reality is our repulsion towards it. For as long as we detest our old reality we are bound to be attached to it, and we will find it hard getting rid of.

That is why we should never fall in the trap of creating a new desirable reality as a reaction towards the old undesirable one. Hostility towards the already existing reality is a clear indication we still have strong ties to it. Repulsion towards the old reality, and every form of attachment to it, can only be overcome by comprehending the fact that we are the sole creators of any reality that hits us, unfavorable realities unconsciously, favorable ones consciously; by understanding the momentary nature of the parallel realities and the role consciousness plays in all of it. To summarize, we lose the old reality and create the new one in the same way: by understanding how any reality originates, and by grasping the role of consciousness in them.

The crucial problem is, therefore, how to free from one's ties and identification with the existing reality, and not how to cross over to another. The transition happens automatically when we cease to identify ourselves with our current one. It is only mental patterns that keep us linked to the existing reality, as well as the attitudes and paradigms – and only the ones that exclude higher consciousness of the parallel realities. Nothing is needed - but we know how strong they can be. They are the only ones that create our reality. They are the only obstacle to our changing our reality. Working with thoughts means that we create new mental patterns that correspond to our new reality and shift in that direction, only temporarily and only mentally.

This will not be a short-lived fantasy: ***the desired state and the new reality are here, but only in our thoughts, only in the element of air***.

In order for this state to materialize, we must download it from the element of air, from the world of ideas and thoughts down to the lower dimensions, lower elements, all the way to the earth. We must connect it with energy, emotions and imagination.

8. WORK WITH WILL AND ENERGY

Thoughts are momentary vibrations in the form of information. In the due process of realization they must assume a more permanent form. We experience it as an intention we wish to carry out, a certain amount of will, determination to persevere, to have a set aim. The realization of any concept or an idea is directly proportional to the extent of this resolution, from the amount of energy vested in the perpetuation against an ever-changing tide. If it stays in its element without the connection to all other elements of *tetragrammaton*, an idea or thought will remain just that – an idea or a thought, and nothing more than that.

The thought being the finest vibration of nature, right above the quantum field, it is close to the very quantum field that exists in the form of pure energy. Energy of the quantum field is static, non-Hertzian, spheric, self-sufficient, and complete. In order for the thought further to develop in its path towards materialization it must unite and fill itself with such energy.

In terms of the *tetragrammaton*, ether and air must unite in order to get to fire.

There are several methods of achieving that, they are an integral part of the spiritual techniques and methods of the disciples and schools of spiritual growth. It is called "magnetic center", where we create the central point or goal we aspire to, that occupies our mind. Associations and people who think alike may bring additional help, schools of thought dedicated to the mutual goal. The monk communities were based on this principle in the past.

When a man works alone on an idea he strays quite easily but still manages to convince himself that he is still on the right track. In spite of the fact that he is mislead he still firmly believes that he is right even though he has not achieved his goal, or he gradually makes do with a less challenging task, and finds ways of rationalizing the situation to himself. He justifies his wrong actions. Man needs assistants, or other people going in the same direction, to keep his focus, so as not to wander off the road. These helpers may introduce corrections in the individual's self-belief system.

If such a commune is unavailable, certain rituals can be of help. That is what prayers were for. Always at the exact same time. As time goes by, rituals tend to turn into an aim unto itself. Prayer was aided by certain objects, religious reading, things symbolizing the purpose, or rosaries that helped focus the mind. Certain ritual clothing or a detail such as an accessory may be useful. For example, certain caps, such as turban, constantly tie our attention to *sahasrara*, the seventh chakra, or the thought focused on God.

To ordinary people any object chosen to represent the goal may be of assistance; an object that will be a constant reminder that at the specific part of the day, the more often the better, he needs to detach himself from his work and surroundings, in order to devote himself to the inner vision and mental formula which will be the definition of the previously chosen desired state or goal. This formula should be repeated for two minutes minimum.

By doing so we discipline our behavior, and our behavior is nothing but the way in which we choose to spend our energy on. If we spend our energy on the things that are not related to our goals, our energy will never lead us to our goal. The old proverbs give us this wisdom that we cannot sit on two chairs at the same time, or serve two masters simultaneously.

We will never achieve anything we want if we are doing something else during that time. We become what we invest our life-energy in, and every investment is preceded by a certain frame of mind. (In the *tetragrammaton* the mental frame is the air, above fire, the energy.) Whether we are aware of it or not, there has always been a frame of mind, in the subtle higher spheres, for anything we have done in our lives, and for everything that has happened to us in our lives. It goes without saying, that it is better to create this frame of mind by ourselves consciously than to suffer the consequences of their unconscious influence.

For the energy to be activated during the process when we repeat the formula of our frame of mind that we have chosen to be our life goal, a concrete life reality may prove to be useful: to bring to awareness the whole outer area of our body. We should stand still, although it can be done while sitting, to join our palms together or just fingers, and to become aware of the whole area of our body, so that by breathing in through the nose we visualize white energy rising from the base of the spine, and up the back, going upward to the back of the head, until it reaches the top of the head.

There it is released by breathing out and letting it splash down our body like a waterfall, completely enwrapping it in the form of light aura. Then, with a new breath moving up in the new round. She filled our thought patterns which repeat.

However, this energy must not be vague, it must personify our goal, it must be felt like passion and thrill we have when we are in the reality we create, when we enjoy it as though it were here and now.

Only the type of energy which burns with our passion, which we feel when we are in our chosen reality, which spontaneously encapsulates and fulfills our entire being, eventually becomes the creative force that changes the reality of our life.

In that fashion we connect the energy of our being with our thoughts. We interconnect ether, air and fire.

That will not be a simple trick played on our mind with thoughts filled with glee. The goal we strive to will be achieved, but only on the level of the air and fire, on the level of mental patterns and the energy of our being.

9. WORK WITH THE IMAGINATION

To be able to develop the process of our realization even further, it will be necessary to position it even lower, to the element of water, meaning to shape it more accurately. It will not be hard, because we have already spent most of our life in fancy rather than in reality, we now only need to add a proper image to our imaginings and to comprehend how it all works, to reach the sphere of consciousness.

Mental image united with energy and intention cannot exist without some form, regardless of the fact how ephemeral it proves to be. Those short-lived forms of our mental patterns we invest our energy into are what we know as imagination. Imagination is an idea turned into an image.

Esoteric science places imagination as an expression of the astral world. It is right above the material world and presents the energy fluid which connects all shapes and runs energy from the higher spheres to the lower. The astral connects pure energy and ideas with a physical shape. Any concrete shaping is rehearsed and prepared on the level of the astral. It is the world of dreams we go to every night in sleep, as we dream.

It is the world we go to when we leave the body. Because it is so close to the physical plain, we see the same or similar to those we see in the material world. But there we can change them at will and create new things, rehearse endless possibilities. For this unfortunate reason the astral has always been the most powerful tool for all magicians and witches to play with, generate all kinds of influences onto the physical plain. Whatever is consciously created in the astral ends up manifested in the physical world, after putting some more appropriate energy into it.

This is why we must shape the mental pattern we have created into some form of vision, image, we must use imagination to bring it to life somehow, so that it seems already accomplished. We should envisage realization so that we can feel it, as if we were in it already. This imagining should be experienced with ecstasy, because it is an expression of fulfillment of the imagined combined with energy. This way we have put together the mental pattern (air) the energy (fire) with the definite image (water) of our desired goal. As if it were already there.

Imagination must be accompanied with a corresponding sensitivity because the element of water that the astral belongs to, also relates to emotions. That is why astral appearances affect our emotions so strongly, people will believe anything and have an adequate emotional response to if it comes from the astral. Thoughts are easier, they change far more quickly, appear and disappear with ease.

The astral affects emotions deeply because that is a very dense area, below the air and fire, it is the plain where mind patterns and energy work together. That is why emotions are so strong and everlasting. Emotion is the same as thought, only joined with energy. Emotion is a more permanent and forceful alteration of a thought. Emotions are thoughts with power and a more durable shape.

We are familiar with all this from our personal experience with the astral, from the nightmares and sad moments, but if we are to understand the basics of emotions, and what imagination truly is, then we can begin to use it as the most powerful tool for creating the reality we want. Every reality, the one we are experiencing included, has been created in the same manner, following the same process. It is wiser to implement it consciously than to suffer at the hand of our unconsciousness.

Working with imagination will be even easier because it is daydreaming with awareness. The method is simple: every day, the more often the better, we should get completely relaxed and disconnect from the reality we are in and picture the reality we wish to live in, with the awareness that we are already in it. With as many details as possible, and more importantly, with a strong sense of accomplishment and joy for having our dreams fulfilled.

If an object is at stake, we should focus in front of us, we should hold it firmly in our hands, and feel it, and if a person is in question, we should see ourselves living with the person the way we want, if this is new ambience for us or the new house, then we should visualize those the tiniest detail, if possible. The key thing here is visualization with all the accompanying details.

It will not be falling for illusions. This desired state is realized, but only to the element of water.

It is going to take another tiny bit for your wish to be materialized in our physical reality.

That minor thing presents bad news for the lazy: we are going to have to work hard physically to be able to get what we want.

10. WORK ON THE PHYSICAL PLAN

The primary law of the physical world is causality. Nothing is derived there from sheer thoughts or ideas (air), or just will and design (water), but by adding up all of these processes, in higher dimensions, we get the desired result on the physical plain. To induce causality which rules the physical plain and achieve the desired result we must connect all the previous processes, from the mental patterns, will and energy to the concrete imagination.

The material world is not just simply one of the elements, it is the sum of ether, air, fire, and water. All of these processes together are projected into what we experience as the physical reality. Physical reality is like the film screen the higher dimensions get projected on. Physical world is the mirror of consciousness.

Only when we bring together all the preceding elements into a unity, when we consistently learn to think in a certain way and with a definite mental pattern, when we invest our energy into it and have a clear and bullet-proof vision of the goal, only then will we actually achieve it.

The law of *tetragrammaton* functions everywhere and in every way, without exceptions. People who explore ideas and the art of writing do so, most dominantly, in the element of air. People who engineer great social change do so in the element of fire. People who deal with the imagination and pictures, virtual reality (painting, film, music, design) and emotions, do this with the element of water prevailingly. People who work with their bodies, and achieve their goal though hard physical work, function mostly in the element of earth.

All the goals during the course of history have been achieved in this fashion: by merging all the elements of the *tetragrammaton* into one harmonious unity.

When we focus our mind on one thing, waste energy on something else, and fantasize about who knows what, we are bound to experience frustration.

All our failures and failed attempts have this chaos in their history.

If you have ever seen a truly realized individual, whether in the mundane or the spiritual sense, then you have observed that this person is always the same, complete, that person possesses a clear and independent mind, clear and independent will and feelings and a unique and clear vision. The person always has one stable I, does not shift own personality under the influence and fluctuations of the outside world. Truly realized individuals always act in accordance with the principles that have formed them and brought them to where they are now.

At the core of all accomplishments in this world the most illustrative is that of a man's self-realization: to be what he is, one personality, not a multitude of split I's.

Man is a microcosm, all the principles and cosmic laws are contained in him. That is why the essence of all accomplishments is that man be what he is, authentic rather than separated from himself. All outer realizations are merely reflections of this inner realization of one's authenticity.

In order for us to change anything and materialize our aspirations, we rely largely on our inner realization, on our inner ability to awaken our mental patterns (air), whether we are aware of this fact and use it consciously or it uses us under an alien or outside influence, and we end up being their slaves; all the expressions of our will and investing the life energy into (fire), whether we use them consciously or they use and enslave us; all emotions, desires and fantasies (water), whether we use them consciously, or end up being used by them and in due course be subjugated by them.

We have seen what tasks lay ahead of us on the plain of thoughts, energy and imagination if we are intent on getting anywhere. This work is actually work on oneself. While we work on ourselves, we get to know ourselves and we end up changing ourselves. This is how we bring awareness to our life, we improve and perfect ourselves. Therefore, all the outer goals are nothing but the indirect means that lead us in the direction of self-awareness, and self-realization. We do not have much use of the outside world if we do not have ourselves.

Be that as it may, a man's life in this world consists of many details. Unlike plants and animals who only have a life, a mere existence, man has a life drama, *karma*, events he participates in, and the events that teach and awaken him to the meaning of everything that exists. For this reason, man gets to know himself, and his true potential, because he is forced to create everything he can create in the visible world, aside the many necessary things, many redundant things as well. Man's self-knowing develops through work and creation in this world, by experiencing everything that can be experienced.

Absolutely everything that he can experience, without limitations. The principle of *tetragrammaton* is best realized in man, because man is god's hand that continues god's work, after the initial creation of nature, the creation through man is continued in the form of all events of life and life drama. Such experience crystallizes the most supreme consciousness in man, of the meaning of existence down to the last detail, of the good, beauty, the right and the wrong. In short, before man, first nature was created, as the existence itself; man, as a conscious subject, experiences all potentials of existence for the purpose of crystallizing consciousness and grasping the meaning of existence.

Therefore, our being, as the principle of the fourfold process of creation, *tetragrammaton*, can and must be used for mundane purposes, not just the spiritual growth. Actually, the very nature of *tetragrammaton* indicates that there is no difference between the two. In the holographic oneness of the universe there are no boundaries, consequently there is none between the outer and the inner world. In man's development, the outer and the inner are complementary.

This practically means that we won't be able to finalize any of our daily tasks if we are unworthy of them. It also means that we reach goals that are undignified because we are like that. We are like that most of the time because we try everything, we have an urge to experience everything. *Tetragrammaton*, like nature itself, acts as a mirror to our consciousness: it always shows us what we are, and it always reflects, confirms, and materializes what we attract with our being and deeds.

The law of causality has effect on entire nature, in all dimensions. The problem is that we do not see beyond the physical plain and we fail to see those aspects of causality that extend to multiple dimensions (water, fire, air, ether). We see only the fragments of this whole process that do not appear to be connected to each other in any way, and then we end up proclaiming these fragments "science" or "laws". That is why many of these things, phenomena, and events seem illogical, unnatural, or unjust, bad or evil. It is only because we do not see the entire process of causality which extends across all the dimensions that we are unable to detect or perceive it with our senses and the physical mind (ego), and that overlaps many of our lives and incarnations.

For this reason it is very important, when realization of an intention of ours is at issue, to keep in mind that our being covers all the dimensions, and not just the physical body, and that our existence is split in many lives, and not just this one we seem to be aware of. It is the real reason why we cannot realize everything here, no matter how hard we try. Some things involve more dimensions and more lives than we know.

How can we rise up to our goals?

More often than not, we should be aware of the entire process of their origin in the form of the fourfold principle of *tetragrammaton* described here. This is the most rudimentary principle of all the existence, of us, our mind, our will, and our feelings. Everything is created in this manner in the outside world. Everything is created in the same way in us. When we harmonize ourselves with the external processes of the origin of everything, only then may we begin to play a part in this process, to start being aware of our capacity towards creating events.

Our work on the material plain mainly consists of comprehending the whole process, firstly, for ourselves, and then through ourselves. If we become aware of it in the proper way our realizations on the physical plain will shortly follow, at the pace objectively needed for the events in the material reality to take form.

Our participation and work on the physical plain is based on the laws of the physical plain itself, and those are inertia and the physical causality, the linear time. The way our former action on the higher plains has formulated the desired outcome, using our thoughts, energy and imagination we must then implement it by working on the physical plain in accordance with the laws of the physical plain. We have to excel in our performance in order for the desired result to materialize, since it had, originally, been envisaged by us.

At the same time we must have the nature of phenomena placed in the correct perspective, especially the nature of time. On higher plains thoughts and imagination change, appear and disappear relatively quickly, while the physical plain is more static. That is why we should not project the manner of work from one plain onto another. Each one has its own characteristics.

On the physical plain the main task is the art of acceptance. Basically, the art of acceptance is understanding how things happen on the physical plain. There is a subtle deception in the very concept of the law of attraction, which leads us to believe that we attract something like magnet, it is just drawn to us. This works only on the higher plains, in the world of ideas and imagination. We can even attract and repel energy. However, on the physical plain there is very little we can attract like a magnet, for it just to fall in our lap. Here we have to achieve everything using our resources maximally.

It is further complicated by the fact that on the physical plain we already have all the things we have formed earlier, and they may obstruct us before we finally reach the desired goal or situation. As previously explained, physical plain is not the right field for the mere projecting of our hopes and wishes because it is largely inert. That is why this is not a clean field, tabula rasa, quite to the contrary, we find here everything that we have projected with our mind, will, and feelings prior to this life, but now wish to change. However, it is not merely we who are the players here, there are also actions of all other conscious subjects who act out their drama in this world. Evidently, our life has been additionally complicated by the things that have been created before. Regardless of this, it can be cleansed and mended, with old obstacles removed, if we have put some conscious effort in constructing our vision on the higher plains.

For this reason, acceptance is the hardest thing. It is much easier just to attract things on the higher plains, mental and emotional. It works instantly. Very often things that do not require some grand physical conditions and resources, such as human relationships, for example, can positively manifest themselves fairly quickly. But if we attract things that require many physical conditions, like material wealth, for instance, numerous pieces of the puzzle will have to fall in place. Money does not fall down from the sky. There are ways of getting it, and we have to do it like that, otherwise money will not come.

That is not going to be the same work as without applying the law of attraction; if we have previously worked on the goal of attracting money on the higher plains, by creating the necessary mental patterns needed for that, by investing energy and imagination, then we have enabled the situation where the road to money will be a lot faster and easier, many doors will open for us, or at least they will no longer be locked. We will have support from the higher dimensions because we have already worked on them, by shaping them to give us support. On this plain, however, we should just follow and accept.

If we need adequate education to get to our goal, we need to go to school; if we want a certain job, we must have the right qualifications, and search for the right employers. If we want a circle of friends of some kind, we must go to the places where such people can be found, where they meet. It is much easier if we take initiative and make the first step, rather than wait for them to come knocking on our door. Although that is also a possibility if we do our part of the job right in the higher plains.

If we want to get healthy we must change the way we live, which, originally, got us in the mess in the first place. We must detoxify ourselves, because every illness is an indication of toxins that are overflowing us, likewise every path to a healthier life would require cleansing our metabolism of various poisons.

It is imperative we choose only accessible goals in the beginning, and not reach for the top, but rather divide our path into smaller sections that are easier to attain. Our first practice would be to exercise with smaller goals. Later on, when our confidence has accumulated, we will find it easier to bite off bigger chunks.

Our realizations are affected by higher plains, our mental paradigms and patterns, our emotional identification of the most profound kind, however, it is important to distinguish between the means and the aim in applying the law of attraction. The best example for this is money. Money is nothing but a means, it can never be the aim in the law of attraction. Our aim must be the sense of accomplishment and pleasure coming from the money well spent, this is what we must visualize and attract, and money will automatically come as a means of achieving the goal. If we focus on money alone, it may happen that we acquire, but completely void of the pleasure it should bring when we spend it on something we love.

Being able to tell the means from the aim apart also means that we should not aspire to some achievement only to run away from something else in our life.

If we are fixated on poverty in our mind, but would like to be rich, on our most subtle, higher plains, with our emotions and mental patterns which are the chief creators of everything, we will be stuck with the idea of poverty, even more emphasized, and it will still be the strongest driving force in the law of attraction. We will continue to have poverty as the only experience in life, nonetheless. Nature is the mirror for our consciousness to reflect in. It shows us what we already have as our mental and emotional capacity on our deepest level, not what we think we want with our superficial minds.

If we aspire to achieve something – because we are in conflict with something else, just to be able to avoid it – we will attract some more of this conflict, rather than what we want. Nature is the mirror, it shows us what we have deep in ourselves, it sees us the way we truly are, down to our essence, and it reflects it for us in the reality of life, regardless of our superficial mind and wishes.

Although we must implement the laws of physical world to accept what we have been attracting on the higher plains, we must not project the laws of higher plains onto the physical world, and we must not project the causality of the physical world onto the higher plains, either. As we have previously stated, causality spans over all the dimensions of nature, although it is not the same everywhere, and the concept of time and space does not apply to it to a large extent.

While creating causes on higher plains, by creating mental patterns, will, and imagination, we must not be driven by the same causality that applies to the physical plain only. This means that we must not ask for means of achieving the ends, we should only ask for the accomplishment of our goal on the higher plains. For example, we first ask for money and all the favorable material aspects for a good marriage and children, and then we work on the marriage and children. On higher plains we must strive towards the chief goal, marital bliss, and this will in turn attract all necessary means for realization, all the money needed, and an appropriate material setting.

When we attract something everything we need for its realization is already included in the package.

THE PROCESS OF REALIZATION

To be worthy of our expectations practically means we should tune in with the prospective environment, to adjust --if not permanently, then temporarily - on occasion. It means going to certain locations, even if they are not part of our reality yet, looking like someone who lives in this reality we are trying to attract, feeling like it, socializing with individuals who are already a part of the reality we are creating.

It may appear to be an imitation at first, but it is actually gradual physical adaptation and the process of getting used to the reality we are trying to attract in our imagination. Physical reality possesses a strong inertia, and it has maximal effect on our habits. That is why it is hardest to overcome the habits that our current reality has imposed on us. We are often conditioned into believing that we cannot change, even when a great new reality is offered to us. That is why in the process of exchanging the old reality for the new we are best served by following the principle – strike fire with fire. We should create a new reality, the one we would like for us to be, occasionally and to a smaller degree, even if it resembled an imitation or a game. Without exaggeration, of course.

Finally, we must be aware of the fact that creativity of the higher dimensions of nature far supersedes our own creativity and our ability to comprehend it. Therefore, its response will always reach us in most fantastic ways. Very rarely will our goals be achieved in the way we imagined it. A practical tip would be never to condition realizations and the way in which our dreams are fulfilled. It poses the biggest challenge to the art of accepting the desired thing.

Because of the very unexpected way in which we get what we have asked for we can be tricked into not recognizing it and even into rejecting it potentially. Sometimes we get bigger and better than we had originally hoped for, and sometimes we get less, because it is for our own good, at this stage of our maturity and development. There are many more people who have discarded gifts of the wholeness, than there are those truly unfortunate and impoverished souls who never got anything.

Creativity of wholeness is best reflected in the fact that not all our aspirations are going to be fulfilled. We are one with the wholeness, intentions and aspirations that are in tune with the self-knowing are the fastest and easiest to come true.

Those aspirations that will harm us or other beings are not likely to come true. Actually, we can achieve those as well, in this universe of free will, but with a lot more effort, repetition, and facing far more numerous warnings on the side of the wholeness that we should mend our ways. Even most negative things are not out of our reach if we are highly dedicated and completely blind to all other options.

A typical characteristic of those who perpetuate their attempt to realize the wrong goals is blind fanaticism. The problem is we are not always aware of what it is that we ask for, and often we dislike what we have been given, or, at best, it sometimes serves the purpose of learning from our mistakes in order to continue growing to a higher level of consciousness, to better options.

The mind we use in the body, and most often make our choices with, is not our only mind, we have a higher mind (higher I), which is connected to the consciousness of our soul, which is one with the wholeness. Many people are deprived in life because their higher mind sees better than the lower mind does, that some of the choices are bad for the individual, and that in the long run they would bring more havoc than good.

Lower mind does not have this perspective so it only sees that its wishes have not been granted. In reality, we use our higher mind to perfect ourselves and our lower egocentric mind.

This way we always get more and better than anything we can ask for. If we could see the divine reality of this existence, of life itself, we would look no further. People who are able to enjoy that illumination always live in a simple and humble way.

To them existence is never unpleasant, it always works well for them. Somehow or other they always have everything they need. They feel wholeness in them and they always feel grateful because they are no different from the wholeness.

Since we, as human beings, are merely conscious subjects of the divine reality that enables everything and that is everything, we realize our aspirations fastest by, once having created the intention and mental vision, we gratefully and lovingly accept absolutely everything that happens to us for we are aware of the fact that the fourfold principle of realization is always present in everything, with or without our intention, and that it works through us and in our favor.

Everything we experience and are aware of happened for that exact reason – for us to experience it and to become aware of it. If there is something we cannot accept unconditionally, it will go on repeating itself into oblivion. Those are the situations we feel trapped in and wish to change with the help of the law of attraction.

They are maintained with our refusal to accept them the way they are, our negativity towards them. Negativity causes a standstill, and positivity instigates change and development. If at the base of some action we have a very negative attitude, then, according to the law of attraction, we will drive it to an even higher degree. That seems like a paradox, but the first step towards the process of changing our reality, without which there is no progress, is accepting with gratitude everything there is here and now – no matter how hard it may seem.

That is the reality we live in, an integral part of absolute reality. We mustn't judge that reality, and debate on whether or not we should accept it, our task is merely to accept it as the reality it is. Our job is to accept it because it was generated in the same way, using the same process we are now trying to change it with. Without accepting the reality it cannot be changed. When we take it for what it is it automatically shifts. As though it had been waiting for the call.

We are conscious subjects of objective reality. Reality would not be possible without the conscious subjects. Therefore, it is there for us, and not vice versa. Comprehending that reality exists for the purpose of our self-awareness is the key to all man's realizations in this world. The illusion that reality is something apart from us, and that we are irrelevant and trapped in it, that we have to fight it, is the essence of slavery and man's suffering. The former is understanding, the latter is illusion.

Our mind is just a tiny fragment of the expression of the wholeness which enables everything. Our mind, our whole being, is already one with it. For that reason, everything we do and accomplish we do unto ourselves; we set on a quest for the awareness of ourselves in everything.

Printed in Great Britain
by Amazon